Easy Lamb Cookbook

50 Delicious Lamb Recipes

By
BookSumo Press

Published by
http://www.booksumo.com

ENJOY THE RECIPES?

KEEP ON COOKING WITH 6 MORE FREE COOKBOOKS!

Click the link below and simply enter your email address to join the club and receive your 6 cookbooks.

LEGAL NOTES

Table of Contents

Norwegian Lamb

Prep Time: 2 h
Total Time: 4 h

Servings per Recipe: 4
Calories	123 kcal
Fat	2 g
Carbohydrates	18.3g
Protein	11 g
Cholesterol	22 mg
Sodium	167 mg

Ingredients

8 oz. sliced lamb meat
1 head cabbage, cored and sliced
2 C. water
1 1/2 tbsps whole black peppercorns
salt to taste

Directions

1. Place on piece of lamb in a Dutch oven or big saucepan then put some cabbage on top.
2. Continue this process of layering lamb and cabbage until all the ingredients have been used up.
3. Now get a cheesecloth and add your peppercorns to it.
4. Tie the cloth with some kitchen string and place the spice bundle to the middle of the layers.
5. Add in your water and place a lid on the pot.
6. Get everything boiling.
7. Once the mix is boiling, set the heat to low and let everything gently cook for 2 hrs.
8. Now discard the cheesecloth and serve.
9. Enjoy.

THYME
and Rosemary Lamb Shanks

🥄 Prep Time: 30 mins

🕐 Total Time: 2 h 30 mins

Servings per Recipe: 6	
Calories	481 kcal
Fat	21.8 g
Carbohydrates	17.6 g
Protein	30.3 g
Cholesterol	93 mg
Sodium	759 mg

Ingredients

6 lamb shanks
salt and pepper to taste
2 tbsps olive oil
2 onions, diced
3 large carrots, cut into 1/4 inch rounds
10 cloves garlic, minced
750 milliliter fish broth

1 (28 oz.) can whole peeled tomatoes with juice
1 (10.5 oz.) can condensed chicken broth
1 (10.5 oz.) can beef broth
5 tsps diced fresh rosemary
2 tsps diced fresh thyme

Directions

1. Coat your lamb with pepper and salt then fry the shanks with a batch process for 10 mins each and place everything to the side.
2. In the same pot begin to stir fry your garlic, carrots, and onions for 12 mins then add: thyme, beef broth, chicken broth, rosemary, tomatoes, and fish broth.
3. Place the lamb back into the pot and get everything boiling.
4. Once the mix is boiling, place a lid on the pot, set the heat to low, and let the contents gently cook for 2 hrs.
5. Now take off the lid and continue cooking everything for 22 more mins then place the lamb in a casserole dish and put the meat in the oven to stay warm.
6. Continue to boil the liquid in the pot until it is thick for about 17 more mins.
7. Coat the lamb with this gravy when ready to serve.
8. Enjoy.

Indian Kebabs

🥣 Prep Time: 15 mins
🕐 Total Time: 2 h 25 mins

Servings per Recipe: 8
Calories   304 kcal
Fat   22.6 g
Carbohydrates   4.7g
Protein   20.1 g
Cholesterol   76 mg
Sodium   665 mg

Ingredients

2 lbs lean ground lamb
2 onions, finely diced
1/2 C. fresh mint leaves, finely diced
1/2 C. cilantro, finely diced
1 tbsp ginger paste
1 tbsp green chili paste
2 tsps ground cumin

2 tsps ground coriander
2 tsps paprika
1 tsp cayenne pepper
2 tsps salt
1/4 C. vegetable oil
skewers

Directions

1. Get a bowl, combine: chili paste, lamb, ginger paste, onions, cilantro, and mint. Add in: salt, cumin, cayenne, paprika, and coriander.
2. Place a covering of plastic on the mix and put everything in the fridge for 2 hrs.
3. Now get your grill hot and oil the grate.
4. With your hands shape the meat into a sausage and stake a skewer through it.
5. Grill these kebabs for 12 mins and turn them every 3 mins.
6. Enjoy.

SOUP OF
Lamb and Tomato

🥣 Prep Time: 20 mins

🕐 Total Time: 1 h 20 mins

Servings per Recipe: 8

Calories	225 kcal
Fat	8.9 g
Carbohydrates	21.1g
Protein	14.4 g
Cholesterol	38 mg
Sodium	800 mg

Ingredients

1 lb ground lamb
1/2 large onion, diced
1 (28 oz.) can diced tomatoes
2 C. water
3 (10.5 oz.) cans beef consommé
1 (10.75 oz.) can condensed tomato soup
4 medium carrots, diced

3 stalks celery, diced
1/2 C. barley
1/2 tsp chili powder
1/2 tsp ground black pepper

Directions

1. Begin to stir fry your onions and lamb.
2. Once the lamb is browned and the onions are see-through remove any resulting oils.
3. Combine in the barley, tomato soup, celery, water, carrots, tomatoes with juice, pepper, chili powder, and consommé.
4. Let the mix cook for 50 mins with a gentle boil.
5. Enjoy.

Classical
Lamb Tagine

Prep Time: 45 mins
Total Time: 10 h 45 mins

Servings per Recipe: 4
Calories	423 kcal
Fat	20.5 g
Carbohydrates	23.6g
Protein	35.8 g
Cholesterol	109 mg
Sodium	1129 mg

Ingredients

3 tbsps olive oil, divided
2 lbs lamb meat, cut into 1 1/2 inch cubes
2 tsps paprika
1/4 tsp ground turmeric
1/2 tsp ground cumin
1/4 tsp cayenne pepper
1 tsp ground cinnamon
1/4 tsp ground cloves
1/2 tsp ground cardamom
1 tsp kosher salt
1/2 tsp ground ginger
1 pinch saffron
3/4 tsp garlic powder

3/4 tsp ground coriander
2 medium onions, cut into 1-inch cubes
5 carrots, peeled, cut into fourths, then sliced
lengthwise into thin strips
3 cloves garlic, minced
1 tbsp freshly grated ginger
1 lemon, zested
1 (14.5 oz.) can homemade chicken broth or
low-sodium canned broth
1 tbsp sun-dried tomato paste
1 tbsp honey
1 tbsp cornstarch (optional)
1 tbsp water (optional)

Directions

1. Get a bowl, combine: coriander, paprika, garlic powder, turmeric, saffron, cumin, ginger, cayenne, salt, cinnamon, cardamom, and cloves.
2. Add in your lamb and work the spices throughout the meat.
3. Now add 2 tbsps of olive oil and coat the lamb with it.
4. Place a covering of plastic on the bowl and put everything in the fridge overnight.
5. Now being to stir fry 1/3 of the lamb in 1 tbsp of olive oil. Once the lamb is brown and done, remove it from the pan, and continue frying the rest in batches.

6. Once all the lamb has been cooked combine in the carrots and onions.

7. Fry everything for 6 mins then add the ginger and garlic.

8. Continue frying everything for 6 more mins.

9. Now add the cooked lamb back to the pot and also add: the honey, lemon zest, tomato paste, and chicken broth.

10. Get everything boiling, place a lid on the pot, set the heat to low, and let the contents cook for 90 mins.

11. Stir the mix every 20 mins.

12. Add some cornstarch and water when 10 mins is left if you find that mix is not thick enough.

13. Enjoy.

Baked
Lamb Shanks

Prep Time: 25 mins
Total Time: 2 h 50 mins

Servings per Recipe: 4
Calories	348 kcal
Fat	15.3 g
Carbohydrates	16.2g
Protein	30.2 g
Cholesterol	89 mg
Sodium	506 mg

Ingredients

1 tbsp vegetable oil
4 lamb shanks
1 onion, diced
4 cloves garlic, diced
2 carrots, diced
2 celery ribs, diced
2 tbsps tomato paste

12 fluid oz. veggie broth
1 (14 oz.) can beef broth
3 sprigs fresh thyme
3 sprigs fresh parsley
1 bay leaf
1 sprig fresh rosemary
salt and pepper to taste

Directions

1. Get your oil hot in a large saucepan then begin to stir fry your lamb for 12 mins then place the meat to the side.
2. Remove any oils from the pot, turn down the heat, and begin to stir fry your garlic and onions for 7 mins.
3. Add in the tomato paste, celery, and onions and cook the veggies for 7 more mins.
4. Now add the lamb back into the pot and also the beef broth and veggie broth.
5. Get this mix boiling, then once it is, set the heat to low and let the contents simmer.
6. Get some kitchen string and tie the following in a bunch: bay leaf, parsley sprigs, and thyme sprigs.
7. Make sure you tie the spices tightly together then add them to the pot.
8. Now place a lid on the pot and cook the mix for 2.5 hrs.
9. Stir the mix every 30 mins and if you find the mix becoming too thick add some water and continue simmering everything.
10. Now add in the pepper, salt, and rosemary when 15 mins of cooking time is left then remove the bunch of herbs and the rosemary.
11. Enjoy.

GREEK
Lamb

Prep Time: 10 mins

Total Time: 1 h

Servings per Recipe: 12
Calories	543 kcal
Fat	29.4 g
Carbohydrates	43.4g
Protein	25.8 g
Cholesterol	172 mg
Sodium	575 mg

Ingredients

24 sheets phyllo dough
4 C. cooked white rice
1 clove garlic, minced
3 C. cubed cooked lamb
1 lemon, juiced
2 potatoes, peeled and quartered
4 hard-cooked eggs, quartered
2 tbsps lemon zest
2 tbsps diced fresh parsley

2 tbsps diced fresh mint leaves
1 1/2 C. crumbled feta cheese
1/2 C. olive oil
1 C. beef broth
1 tbsp diced fresh oregano
1/2 tsp ground black pepper
1 egg, beaten
1/2 C. butter, melted

Directions

1. Set your oven to 325 degrees before doing anything else.
2. Get your potatoes boiling in water and salt for 17 mins then remove all the liquids and dice the potatoes once they have lost their heat.
3. Now coat a casserole dish with melted butter and lay one piece of phyllo.
4. Coat the sheet of phyllo with some more melted butter then keep adding layers in this manner for 12 sheets.
5. Add some rice over the sheets of pastry then some garlic and lamb.
6. Make sure the phyllo is evenly covered with lamb then add some lemon juice over everything.
7. Now set your oven to 325 degrees before doing anything else.
8. Get your potatoes and add a layer of diced potatoes over the lamb.

9. Place your egg pieces and top of the potatoes with: the feta, parsley, lemon zest, and mint.
10. Coat everything with the beef broth and olive oil.
11. Season the layers with some pepper and oregano then add the whisked eggs.
12. Finally add the last 12 sheets of pastry and coat everything with more melted butter.
13. Cook the layers in the oven for 45 mins.
14. When 10 mins are left increase oven to 350 degrees.
15. Slice the layers into rectangles or squares before serving.
16. Enjoy.

IRISH
Lamb Pot Roast

Prep Time: 20 mins
Total Time: 2 h 45 mins

Servings per Recipe: 10

Calories	672 kcal
Fat	39.3 g
Carbohydrates	26.3g
Protein	46.4 g
Cholesterol	163 mg
Sodium	1189 mg

Ingredients

1 1/2 lbs thickly sliced turkey bacon, diced
6 lbs boneless lamb shoulder, cut into 2 inch pieces
1/2 tsp salt
1/2 tsp ground black pepper
1/2 C. all-purpose flour
3 cloves garlic, minced
1 large onion, diced
1/2 C. water

4 C. beef stock
2 tsps white sugar
4 C. diced carrots
2 large onions, cut into bite-size pieces
3 potatoes
1 tsp dried thyme
2 bay leaves
1 C. fish broth

Directions

1. Fry your bacon.
2. Once it is done break it into pieces and place it to the side.
3. Get a bowl, combine: flour, lamb, pepper, and salt.
4. Mix everything with your hands then brown the meat in the drippings from the bacon.
5. Once the meat is browned add it into a saucepan.
6. Begin to fry your onions and garlic in the fat until the onions are brown. Then add half a C. of water to the onions and stir everything.
7. Now pour the mix into the saucepan and add the sugar, beef stock, and bacon to the pan as well.
8. Get everything boiling.
9. Once the mix is boiling set the heat to medium / low and let the contents gently cook for 90 mins.
10. Now stir in the fish broth, carrots, bay leaves, onions, thyme, and potatoes.
11. Set the heat lower and continue cooking everything for 25 more mins.
12. Enjoy.

Rosemary Dijon
Rack of Lamb

Prep Time: 20 mins
Total Time: 2 h 25 mins

Servings per Recipe: 4

Calories	481 kcal
Fat	40.8 g
Carbohydrates	5.6g
Protein	22.2 g
Cholesterol	94 mg
Sodium	1369 mg

Ingredients

1/2 C. fresh bread crumbs
2 tbsps minced garlic
2 tbsps diced fresh rosemary
1 tsp salt
1/4 tsp black pepper
2 tbsps olive oil
1 (7 bone) rack of lamb, trimmed and frenched

1 tsp salt
1 tsp black pepper
2 tbsps olive oil
1 tbsp Dijon mustard

Directions

1. Set your oven to 450 degrees before doing anything else.
2. Get a bowl, combine: 1/4 tsp pepper, bread crumbs, 1 tsp salt, garlic, and rosemary.
3. Stir the mix then add 2 tbsp of olive oil and stir everything again.
4. Coat your lamb with pepper and salt.
5. Then begin to get some olive oil hot in a frying pan.
6. With a high level of heat sear the meat for 3 mins all over then place the lamb to the side for 3 mins.
7. Top the meat first with mustard and then coat it with the bread crumb mix.
8. Place a covering of foil on the ends of the lamb then place the lamb with the bones facing downwards in the frying pan.
9. Put everything in the oven to cook for 15 mins.
10. Enjoy.

EGYPTIAN
Lamb

🥣 Prep Time: 45 mins

🕐 Total Time: 1 h 20 mins

Servings per Recipe: 28

Calories	35 kcal
Fat	2.3 g
Carbohydrates	0.6g
Protein	< 2.9 g
Cholesterol	11 mg
Sodium	78 mg

Ingredients

4 cloves garlic, minced
1 tsp kosher salt
1 lb ground lamb
3 tbsps grated onion
3 tbsps diced fresh parsley
1 tbsp ground coriander
1 tsp ground cumin
1/2 tbsp ground cinnamon

1/2 tsp ground allspice
1/4 tsp cayenne pepper
1/4 tsp ground ginger
1/4 tsp ground black pepper
28 bamboo skewers, soaked in water for 30 minutes

Directions

1. Grab a mortar and pestle and work your salt and garlic into a paste.
2. Get a bowl, combine: pepper, garlic paste, ginger, onions, cayenne, parsley, allspice, coriander, cinnamon, and cumin.
3. Add the lamb and work the mix with your hands so the spices are evenly incorporated into the meat.
4. Now shape your lamb into 25 meatballs then stake each ball onto a skewer and shape the meat into a sausage.
5. Continue making kebabs in this manner until all the ingredients have been used up.
6. Lay all your kebabs in a casserole dish and cover the dish with some plastic.
7. Put everything in the fridge for 1 hr.
8. Get your grill hot and coat the grate with oil.
9. Cook your kebabs on the grill for 8 mins.
10. Enjoy.

Classical
Lamb for Gyros

Prep Time: 15 mins
Total Time: 2 h

Servings per Recipe: 10
Calories	179 kcal
Fat	11.7 g
Carbohydrates	1.9g
Protein	< 15.7 g
Cholesterol	59 mg
Sodium	97 mg

Ingredients

1/2 onion, cut into chunks
1 lb ground lamb
1 lb ground beef
1 tbsp minced garlic
1 tsp dried oregano
1 tsp ground cumin
1 tsp dried marjoram

1 tsp ground dried rosemary
1 tsp ground dried thyme
1 tsp ground black pepper
1/4 tsp sea salt

Directions

1. Blend your onions with a few pulses to finely grind them.
2. Place the onions into some paper towel and squeeze everything together to remove any liquids.
3. Get a bowl, combine: beef, salt, garlic, black pepper, oregano, thyme, cumin, rosemary, and marjoram, lamb, and onions.
4. Combine the mix with your hands then place a covering of plastic on the bowl and put everything in the fridge for 90 mins.
5. Now set your oven to 325 degrees before doing anything else.
6. Grab your blender again and begin to pulse the meat for about 50 secs.
7. Enter the meat into a bread pan then place a moist kitchen towel in a roasting pan. Layer the bread pan on top of the towel and put everything in the oven.
8. Pour boiling water into the roasting pan until half of the pan is filled with water then cook the meat in the oven for 55 mins.
9. Remove any excess oils then carve the meat.
10. Enjoy.

BALSAMIC
Lamb Chops

Prep Time: 10 mins
Total Time: 40 mins

Servings per Recipe: 4
Calories	257 kcal
Fat	19.4 g
Carbohydrates	5.2g
Protein	14.7 g
Cholesterol	65 mg
Sodium	347 mg

Ingredients

3/4 tsp dried rosemary
1/4 tsp dried basil
1/2 tsp dried thyme
salt and pepper to taste
4 lamb chops (3/4 inch thick)
1 tbsp olive oil
1/4 C. minced shallots
1/3 C. aged balsamic vinegar

3/4 C. chicken broth
1 tbsp butter

Directions

1. Get a bowl, combine: pepper, rosemary, salt, thyme, and basil.
2. Coat your pieces of lamb evenly with this mix.
3. Place the lamb in a dish and place a covering of plastic over everything.
4. Put the meat in the fridge for 30 mins.
5. Now begin to fry your lamb in olive oil for 5 mins each side or more if you prefer the meat to be more done.
6. Remove everything from the pan and then begin to stir fry your shallots for 2 mins then add the vinegar and scrape the pan.
7. After scraping the pan add in your broth and cook everything for 7 mins.
8. At this point half of the liquid should have evaporated, if not, continue simmering it.
9. Once only half of the sauce remains shut the heat and add in your butter.
10. Top your pieces of lamb with this sauce.
11. Enjoy.

Greek
Lamb II

Prep Time: 25 mins
Total Time: 1 h

Servings per Recipe: 4
Calories   694 kcal
Fat   32.9 g
Carbohydrates   66.6 g
Protein   32.5 g
Cholesterol   95 mg
Sodium   2952 mg

Ingredients

1 tbsp olive oil
1 lb ground lamb
6 cloves garlic, crushed
1 large onion, sliced
1 tbsp dried oregano
2/3 tsp ground cumin
2 tsps salt
2 tsps freshly ground black pepper

1 dash hot pepper sauce
2/3 C. diced fresh parsley
1 lb pizza crust dough
6 oz. feta cheese
1/2 zucchini, diced
8 oz. diced black olives
1/2 tsp garlic powder

Directions

1. Set your oven to 450 degrees before doing anything else.
2. Begin to brown the meat in hot oil along with: hot sauce, garlic, pepper, onions, salt, cumin, and oregano.
3. When the lamb is basically cooked add the parsley and continue cooking everything for 2 more mins.
4. Now place everything to the side.
5. Shape your dough into a large rectangle.
6. Layer the following on the dough evenly: olives, feta, and zucchini.
7. Try to leave some space on the edge of the dough.
8. Now add the lamb mix once it has lost all of its heat and roll everything up.
9. Seal the roll by crimping the edge.
10. Coat the entire roll with garlic powder and bake it in the oven for 7 mins then lower the oven to 350 degrees and cook the dish for 30 more mins.
11. Enjoy.

EASY
Lamb Chops

🥄 Prep Time: 10 mins
🕐 Total Time: 55 mins

Servings per Recipe: 6
Calories	738 kcal
Fat	45.2 g
Carbohydrates	26.7g
Protein	52.4 g
Cholesterol	1270 mg
Sodium	462 mg

Ingredients

3 eggs
3 tsps Worcestershire sauce
12 (5.5 oz.) lamb chops
2 C. dry bread crumbs

Directions

1. Set your oven to 375 degrees before doing anything else.
2. Get a bowl, combine: Worcestershire and eggs.
3. Whisk the mix until it is all smooth then coat your lamb with the mix and some bread crumbs.
4. Place everything into a casserole dish and cook the meat in the oven for 22 mins.
5. Now flip the lamb chops and cook them for 22 more mins.
6. Enjoy.

Sweet
Brown Sugar Lamb

Prep Time: 15 mins
Total Time: 2 h 25 mins

Servings per Recipe: 4
Calories   241 kcal
Fat   13.1 g
Carbohydrates   15.8g
Protein   14.6 g
Cholesterol   56 mg
Sodium   339 mg

Ingredients

1/4 C. brown sugar
2 tsps ground ginger
2 tsps dried tarragon
1 tsp ground cinnamon
1 tsp ground black pepper
1 tsp garlic powder
1/2 tsp salt

4 lamb chops

Directions

1. Get a bowl, combine: salt, brown sugar, garlic powder, ginger, pepper, cinnamon, and tarragon.
2. Coat your pieces of lamb with this mix then place everything in a dish.
3. Cover the dish with plastic and place everything in the fridge for 2 hrs.
4. Now get your grill hot and coat the grate with oil.
5. Cook your pieces of lamb for 5 mins per side.
6. Enjoy.

MEDITERRANEAN
Meatballs

Prep Time: 10 mins
Total Time: 20 mins

Servings per Recipe: 8
Calories	185 kcal
Fat	13.7 g
Carbohydrates	1.5g
Protein	< 13.8 g
Cholesterol	98 mg
Sodium	482 mg

Ingredients

1 lb ground lamb
1/2 C. diced fresh parsley
2 tbsps finely diced onion
1/2 C. crumbled feta cheese
1/2 C. diced green olives
2 eggs
1 tsp Italian seasoning

Directions

1. Turn on your oven's broiler.
2. Get a bowl, combine: Italian seasoning, lamb, eggs, parsley, olives, feta, and onions.
3. Form the meat into 16 balls of an even size and lay them all in a casserole dish.
4. Cook the lamb under the broiler until the top is browned then flip the balls and cook the opposite end.
5. Enjoy.

Algerian
Lamb Soup

Prep Time: 15 mins
Total Time: 2 h 45 mins

Servings per Recipe: 6	
Calories	467 kcal
Fat	16.7 g
Carbohydrates	50g
Protein	29.4 g
Cholesterol	116 mg
Sodium	594 mg

Ingredients

1 lb cubed lamb meat
1 tsp ground turmeric
1 1/2 tsps ground black pepper
1 tsp ground cinnamon
1/4 tsp ground ginger
1/4 tsp ground cayenne pepper
2 tbsps margarine
3/4 C. diced celery
1 onion, diced

1 red onion, diced
1/2 C. diced fresh cilantro
1 (29 oz.) can diced tomatoes
7 C. water
3/4 C. green lentils
1 (15 oz.) can garbanzo beans, drained
4 oz. vermicelli pasta
2 eggs, beaten
1 lemon, juiced

Directions

1. Heat and stir the following in a saucepan for 7 mins: cilantro, lamb, onion, turmeric, celery, black pepper, butter, cayenne, cinnamon, and ginger.
2. Add in the tomatoes with juice, set the heat to low, and gently cook the mix for 17 more mins.
3. Now add in the water and lentils.
4. Stir everything then get it all boiling.
5. Once the mix is boiling place, place a lid on the pot, set the heat to low, and let the contents gently cook for 2 hrs.
6. Once 15 mins of cooking time is left increase the heat and add in the noodles and chickpeas.
7. Continue simmering everything for the remaining time then add in the eggs and lemon.
8. Cook everything for 3 more mins.
9. Enjoy.

LAMB
on the Grill

Prep Time: 10 mins
Total Time: 3 h 16 mins

Servings per Recipe: 6
Calories	519 kcal
Fat	44.8 g
Carbohydrates	2.3g
Protein	< 25 g
Cholesterol	112 mg
Sodium	861 mg

Ingredients

1/4 C. distilled white vinegar
2 tsps salt
1/2 tsp black pepper
1 tbsp minced garlic
1 onion, thinly sliced
2 tbsps olive oil
2 lbs lamb chops

Directions

1. Get a bowl, combine: olive oil, vinegar, onion, salt, garlic, and pepper.
2. Stir the mix then add in the lamb and stir everything again.
3. Place a covering of plastic on the bowl and put everything in the fridge for 3 hrs.
4. Now get your grill hot and coat the grate with oil.
5. Take out your lamb and add some foil to the ends of it to shield the bones from direct heat.
6. Cook the meat on the grill for 4 mins each.

NOTE: If you prefer to avoid grilling. Cook the lamb with your oven's broiler for about 6 mins each side.

Feta
Lamb Burgers

🥣 Prep Time: 15 mins
🕐 Total Time: 25 mins

Servings per Recipe: 4
Calories   478 kcal
Fat   22.4 g
Carbohydrates   38g
Protein   29.4 g
Cholesterol   101 mg
Sodium   1003 mg

Ingredients

1 lb ground lamb
2 tbsps diced fresh mint leaves
2 tbsps diced fresh cilantro
2 tbsps diced fresh oregano
1 tbsp garlic, diced
1 tsp sherry
1 tsp white wine vinegar
1 tsp molasses

1 tsp ground cumin
1/4 tsp ground allspice
1/2 tsp red pepper flakes
1/2 tsp salt
1/2 tsp ground black pepper
4 pita bread rounds
4 oz. feta cheese, crumbled

Directions

1. Get a bowl, combine: molasses, mint, vinegar, cilantro, sherry, oregano, and garlic.

2. Stir the mix then add in black pepper, cumin, salt, allspice, and pepper flakes.

3. Stir the mix then shape everything into 4 burgers.

4. Cook the burgers on the grill for 6 mins each side.

5. Now toast your pieces of pita and fill them with the feta.

6. Enjoy.

POMEGRANATES
and Lamb

 Prep Time: 15 mins

Total Time: 2 h 45 mins

Servings per Recipe: 6

Calories	546 kcal
Fat	34.1 g
Carbohydrates	23.3g
Protein	34.9 g
Cholesterol	134 mg
Sodium	113 mg

Ingredients

3 lbs lamb shoulder blade chops
salt and freshly ground pepper to taste
1 tbsp vegetable oil
1 onion, sliced
1 pinch salt
4 cloves garlic, sliced
2 C. pomegranate juice
1/3 C. aged balsamic vinegar

1/4 tsp dried rosemary
8 fresh mint leaves
1/4 tsp red pepper flakes
1 tbsp honey, or more to taste
salt and ground black pepper to taste
2 tbsps pomegranate seeds
1 tbsp sliced fresh mint leaves
1 tbsp pumpkin seeds

Directions

1. Set your oven to 300 degrees before doing anything else. Then coat your lamb with pepper and salt.
2. Brown the meat in veggie oil for 9 mins then place the meat to the side.
3. Now turn the heat down to medium and being to stir fry your onions with some salt for 5 mins then add in the garlic and fry it for 1 more mins.
4. Add the pomegranate juice and scrape the pan.
5. Now add the balsamic and turn up the heat to a high level.
6. Get everything boiling then add in: the pepper flakes, rosemary, and mint leaves.
7. Let the mix continue to cook for 12 mins then add the lamb and its drippings.
8. Cover the lamb with the sauce in the pot and place a lid over everything.
9. Let the mix cook for 2 hrs with a low heat.
10. Remove the lamb from the pot. Then turn up the heat again.
11. Let the sauce boil for 6 mins then add some black pepper, salt, and the honey.
12. Add the lamb back in and stir everything.
13. Top the dish with some pumpkin seeds, mint, and pomegranate seeds.
14. Enjoy.

Lamb
Biryani

🍲 Prep Time: 25 mins
🕐 Total Time: 1 hr 25 mins

Servings per Recipe: 8
Calories   544 kcal
Fat   25 g
Carbohydrates   64.3g
Protein   16.5 g
Cholesterol   43 mg
Sodium   410 mg

Ingredients

2 1/2 C. basmati rice
1/4 C. cooking oil
8 whole cloves
4 black cardamom pods
4 cinnamon sticks
4 large onions, sliced thin
1 tbsp garlic paste
1 tbsp ginger paste
1/4 C. diced fresh cilantro leaves
3 tbsps diced fresh mint leaves
1 lb lamb chops
salt to taste

3 tomatoes, diced
4 green chili peppers, halved lengthwise
2 tsps ground red pepper
2 tbsps plain yogurt
2 tbsps lemon juice
7 1/2 C. water
1 tsp salt
1 tbsp vegetable oil
1 onion, sliced
1/2 tsp saffron
2 tbsps warm milk

Directions

1. Let your rice sit submerged in water for 40 mins.
2. Now get 1/4 C. of oil hot and stir fry your cinnamon sticks, cardamom, and cloves for 2 mins.
3. Combine in the onions, cook them for 7 mins. Then add the ginger paste and garlic.
4. Cook the mix for 2 mins then add the mint and cilantro.
5. Cook the spice for 30 secs.
6. Combine in the lamb pieces and top them with salt.
7. Fry the lamb for 22 mins then add: the ground red pepper, chili pepper, and tomatoes.
8. Let this mix fry for 12 mins then stir in the lemon juice and yogurt.
9. Place a lid on the pot and cook everything for 17 mins.

10. Now get your basmati boiling in 1 tsp of salt and 7.5 C. of water.
11. Let the rice boil for 12 mins. Then remove all the liquids which are left over.
12. Stir fry your onions in a separate pot in 1 tbsp of oil until brown.
13. Get a new sauce pan and add half of the rice to it. Top the rice with the lamb mix then add the onions.
14. Now add the rest of the rice and place a lid on the pot.
15. Let the contents gently cook for 17 mins with a low level of heat.
16. Enjoy.

Dijon
Pistachio Lamb

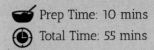 Prep Time: 10 mins

Total Time: 55 mins

Servings per Recipe: 4

Calories	619 kcal
Fat	39.8 g
Carbohydrates	10.3g
Protein	53.1 g
Cholesterol	1164 mg
Sodium	768 mg

Ingredients

2 racks of lamb, trimmed
1 tsp herbes de Provence
salt and ground black pepper to taste
1 tbsp vegetable oil
2/3 C. diced pistachio nuts
2 tbsps dry bread crumbs
1 tbsp melted butter
1 tsp olive oil

salt and ground black pepper to taste
3 tbsps Dijon mustard

Directions

1. Cover a cookie sheet with foil then set your oven to 400 degrees before doing anything else.
2. Coat your lamb with black pepper, salt, and Herbes de Provence.
3. Now fry your lamb for 7 mins per side then place the meat on the cookie sheet.
4. Get a bowl, combine: black pepper, pistachios, salt, bread crumbs, olive oil, and butter.
5. Coat the fatty side of your lamb with mustard then place the bread crumb mix on top of the mustard.
6. Cook everything in the oven for 22 mins.
7. Enjoy.

GRILLED LAMB
with Mushrooms

Prep Time: 20 mins
Total Time: 1 hr

Servings per Recipe: 4
Calories	351 kcal
Fat	27.7 g
Carbohydrates	2.4g
Protein	< 22.8 g
Cholesterol	77 mg
Sodium	531 mg

Ingredients

2 tbsps olive oil
1 (8 oz.) package sliced fresh mushrooms
8 slices turkey bacon
4 lamb blade chops
1 tsp cracked black peppercorns
seasoned salt to taste

Directions

1. Get your grill hot then coat the grate with oil.
2. Begin to stir fry your mushrooms in olive oil until they are soft.
3. Now top your bacon with pepper and grill them until crispy on both sides.
4. Coat your pieces of lamb with salt and grill the meat for about 5 mins per side.
5. Top the lamb with mushrooms and bacon.
6. Enjoy.

Mint
Radish Lamb

🥄 Prep Time: 10 mins
🕐 Total Time: 3 h 45 mins

Servings per Recipe: 4
Calories   530 kcal
Fat   36.2 g
Carbohydrates   9.1g
Protein   39.4 g
Cholesterol   158 mg
Sodium   1759 mg

Ingredients

1 tbsp kosher salt
1 tsp black pepper
1 tsp paprika
1/4 tsp cayenne pepper
4 (10 oz.) lamb shoulder chops
1 tbsp olive oil
1/3 C. sherry vinegar
2 tbsps white sugar

4 oil-packed anchovy fillets
1 1/2 C. low-sodium chicken broth
2 tsps minced fresh rosemary
1/4 tsp ground cinnamon
2 bunches breakfast radishes, rinsed and trimmed
5 fresh mint leaves, finely sliced
1 tbsp cold butter

Directions

1. Set your oven to 275 degrees before doing anything else.
2. Coat your pieces of lambs with cayenne, salt, paprika, and pepper.
3. Fry the lamb in hot oil for 5 mins each side then place the meat to the side.
4. Set the heat to low and combine in the pot: anchovies, sugar, and vinegar.
5. Stir the mix, crumble the anchovies, and increase the heat.
6. Cook everything for 4 mins. Then add the broth and turn up the heat.
7. Now add in the cinnamon and rosemary.
8. Get everything boiling then add the lamb back into the mix with the radishes. Place a lid on the pot and set the heat to a lower level.
9. Let the mix cook for 90 mins. Then flip the lamb and cook it for 17 more mins.
10. Place the radishes and meat on a dish and simmer the sauce for more time until it becomes thick.
11. Remove any extra fats from the sauce then add in the butter and mint.
12. Let the butter melt then top the lamb with the mix.
13. Enjoy.

INDIAN
Lamb II

🥣 Prep Time: 30 mins
🕐 Total Time: 3 hr 30 mins

Servings per Recipe: 6
Calories	450 kcal
Fat	24.9 g
Carbohydrates	16.1g
Protein	21.9 g
Cholesterol	77 mg
Sodium	357 mg

Ingredients

1/4 C. olive oil
2 lbs boneless lamb shoulder, cut into 2 inch pieces
salt and ground black pepper to taste
1 onion, cut into small dice
1 celery rib, cut into small dice
1 carrot, cut into small dice
1/2 large fennel bulb, cut into small dice
4 cloves garlic, thinly sliced
1 (28 oz.) can Italian-style peeled tomatoes (such as

Cento(R) San Marzano), crushed by hand
2 1/2 C. broth
4 sprigs fresh marjoram
3 sprigs fresh thyme
1 sprig fresh rosemary
3 C. water, divided, or more as needed
3 sprigs rosemary, leaves stripped and diced
1 orange, zested
1 tsp red pepper flakes

Directions

1. Coat your lamb with pepper and salt then brown it for 25 mins, in olive oil, in a large pot. Then place the lamb aside.
2. Now set your oven to 350 degrees before doing anything else.
3. Stir the fry the following in the lamb drippings: garlic, onions, fennel, celery, and carrots.
4. Add in some salt and fry the mix for 12 more mins.
5. Add the lamb back into the pot and pour in the broth and tomatoes.
6. Now get a kitchen string and tightly bind the following together in a bundle: rosemary, thyme, and marjoram.
7. Add the bundle to the pot and place a lid over everything.
8. Get the mix boiling for 2 mins then place everything in the oven for 65 mins.
9. Add 1 cup of water to mix and cook the contents for 65 more mins.
10. Now take out the meat and slice it into bite sized pieces then add it back to the pot with another C. of water.
11. Let everything cook for 35 more mins then add the pepper flakes, orange zest, and rosemary.
12. Enjoy.

Lamb
Leg
(Dump Dinner)

Prep Time: 10 mins
Total Time: 7 hr 25 mins

Servings per Recipe: 6
Calories	285 kcal
Fat	14 g
Carbohydrates	10.5g
Protein	25.6 g
Cholesterol	100 mg
Sodium	465 mg

Ingredients

1 (3 lb) bone-in leg of lamb, or more to taste
1/2 C. broth
1 lemon, juiced
2 tbsps raw honey
2 tbsps Dijon mustard
3 cloves garlic, minced
1 tbsp apple cider vinegar
1 tbsp dried rosemary

1 tsp dried thyme
1 tsp sea salt
1/2 tsp fresh cracked pepper

Directions

1. Let your lamb sit for 3 hrs on a counter top in a bowl.
2. Add your broth to the crock of a slow cooker.
3. Now get a bowl, combine: pepper, lemon juice, salt, honey, thyme, rosemary, mustard, vinegar, and garlic.
4. Stir the mix until it becomes paste like then coat your lamb with the mix.
5. Place everything into the crock pot and cook the contents for 5 hrs with a low level of heat.
6. Enjoy.

GRAPE LEAVES
and Lamb

Prep Time: 45 mins
Total Time: 1 hr 30 mins

Servings per Recipe: 8
Calories	250 kcal
Fat	16.1 g
Carbohydrates	18.1g
Protein	9.8 g
Cholesterol	45 mg
Sodium	2485 mg

Ingredients

1/2 lb ground lamb
1/2 C. uncooked long grain rice
1/4 C. olive oil
2 tbsps diced fresh mint
1 tbsp dried currants
1 tbsp pine nuts
1 1/2 tsps kosher salt
1 tsp ground black pepper
1/2 tsp ground cumin

1/4 tsp ground cinnamon
1/4 tsp dried oregano
1 large egg
1 (16 oz.) jar grape leaves
1 tbsp olive oil
juice of one lemon
4 C. hot chicken broth
2 tsps olive oil, or as desired

Directions

1. Get a bowl, combine: eggs, lamb, oregano, rice, cinnamon, 1/4 C. olive oil, cumin, mint, pepper, salt, pine nuts, and currants.

2. Combine the mix evenly then place a covering of plastic on the bowl and put everything in the fridge.

3. Rinse your grapes leaves after separating them under water and place a few leaves to the side for later.

4. Lay out the rest of the leaves then put a tbsp of lamb mix in the middle of each.

5. Fold the edges in, then roll the leaves.

6. Coat a saucepan with 1 tbsp of olive oil then layer the leaves you placed to the side in the pot.

7. Try to make 2 layers.

8. Now layer your rolled leaves and try to make two levels of them. Coat everything with 2 tsps of

olive oil and some lemon juice.

9. Combine in your broth and get everything gently boiling with a medium level of heat and once everything is simmering set the heat to low and place a lid on the pot.

10. Let the rolls cook for 40 mins.

11. Enjoy.

LAMB
Chili

Prep Time: 10 mins
Total Time: 40 mins

Servings per Recipe: 4
Calories	571 kcal
Fat	18.5 g
Carbohydrates	65.1g
Protein	40.1 g
Cholesterol	76 mg
Sodium	3049 mg

Ingredients

1 lb ground lamb
1/2 C. onion, diced
1 clove garlic, minced
2 (15 oz.) cans black beans, rinsed and drained
3 C. canned tomato sauce
1 (14.5 oz.) can diced tomatoes
1/2 (15 oz.) can refried black beans

1 (7 oz.) can diced green chilies
2 tbsps cocoa powder
1 1/2 tbsps chili powder
2 tsps ground cumin
1 cube chicken bouillon, crushed
1/2 tsp cayenne pepper

Directions

1. Stir fry your garlic, onions, and lamb for 9 mins then add in: cayenne, black beans, bouillon, tomato sauce, cumin, diced tomatoes, chili powder, refried beans, cocoa, and green chilies.

2. Let the mix simmer for 25 mins.

3. Enjoy.

Milanese
Lamb

Prep Time: 15 mins
Total Time: 6 h 35 mins

Servings per Recipe: 4
Calories	479 kcal
Fat	20.2 g
Carbohydrates	23.3g
Protein	36.7 g
Cholesterol	128 mg
Sodium	439 mg

Ingredients

1/2 C. all-purpose flour
2 1/2 lbs lamb shanks
salt and freshly ground black pepper to taste
2 tbsps unsalted butter
1 C. broth
1 (14.5 oz.) can diced tomatoes
1 1/2 C. diced onion
3/4 C. chicken broth

1/2 C. diced celery
5 sprigs fresh thyme, leaves removed

Directions

1. Coat your lamb with pepper and salt then coat the meat with flour.
2. Fry your lamb in butter for 6 mins each side then place the meat in the crock of a slow cooker.
3. Now get your broth boiling and scrape the pan then add the broth into the crock as well.
4. Combine in: the thyme, tomatoes with liquid, celery, onions, and broth.
5. Let the mix cook with a low heat for 7 hrs.
6. Place the meat on a serving dish and wrap it with foil.
7. Now gently boil the drippings in the crock pot in a pan for 13 mins until only about 2 C. is left.
8. Then add some pepper and salt.
9. Top the lamb with this sauce when serving.
10. Enjoy.

ALGERIAN
Lamb II

Prep Time: 30 mins
Total Time: 3 h 30 mins

Servings per Recipe: 8	
Calories	375 kcal
Fat	22.5 g
Carbohydrates	24.3g
Protein	20.9 g
Cholesterol	62 mg
Sodium	835 mg

Ingredients

2 large tomatoes, cut into chunks
2 onions, cut into chunks
1 serrano pepper, cut into chunks
1 Anaheim pepper, cut into chunks
1/2 zucchini, cut into chunks
3 cloves garlic
1/4 C. olive oil
1 lb lamb stew meat, cut into 1-inch cubes
3/4 lb ground beef
2 tsps salt
2 cubes vegetable bouillon, or more to taste
2 tsps ground cumin

1 tsp ground black pepper
1 tsp paprika
1/2 tsp ground coriander
1/4 tsp ground turmeric
1/4 tsp cayenne pepper
2 1/2 quarts water
1 (6 oz.) can tomato paste
1/2 C. finely ground freekeh
2 C. green peas
2 tbsps butter
1 bunch cilantro, coarsely diced
1 lemon, cut into wedges, or more to taste

Directions

1. Puree the following until smooth: garlic, tomatoes, zucchini, onions, Anaheim, and serrano.
2. Now begin to fry your beef and lamb in olive oil for a few mins then add in some salt.
3. Cook this mix for 27 mins stirring it at least 3 times.
4. Add the following to the meat: cayenne, puree, turmeric, bouillon, coriander, cumin, paprika, and black pepper.
5. Get everything boiling, then set the heat to low, and let the contents gently cook for 40 mins. Then add in the tomato paste and water.
6. Get the mix simmering again and continue cooking it for 90 mins.

7. Now add in your freekeh and cook everything for 35 more mins.
8. Finally add the butter and peas.
9. Shut the heat and top everything with your cilantro and some freshly squeeze lemon juice.
10. Enjoy.

EASY
Lamb Korma (Indian Style)

Prep Time: 10 mins
Total Time: 1 hr 25 mins

Servings per Recipe: 6

Calories	301 kcal
Fat	13.8 g
Carbohydrates	17.4g
Protein	28.1 g
Cholesterol	80 mg
Sodium	102 mg

Ingredients

2 1/4 lbs cubed lamb meat
4 tsps olive oil, divided
1 brown onion, diced
1 red potato, peeled and cubed
1/2 C. curry powder
1/2 C. water
1/3 C. coconut milk

1/3 C. drained canned chickpeas (garbanzo beans)

Directions

1. Get a bowl, combine: lamb and 2 tsps of olive oil.
2. Stir the mix to evenly coat the meat.
3. Now begin to stir fry your onions in 2 tbsps of olive for 12 mins then shut the heat and add the potatoes.
4. Begin to fry your lamb in a separate pot 1/4 at a time for about 7 mins for each batch.
5. Place the lamb once it is browned with the potatoes.
6. Continue frying your lamb in this manner until all of it is cooked then add it with the potatoes.
7. Add the curry to the lamb and potatoes mix, stir everything, then heat it all for 2 mins.
8. Now pour in some water and get everything boiling.
9. Set the heat to low, place a lid on the pot, and let the contents cook for 50 mins.
10. Stir in the chickpeas and coconut milk and cook everything for about 7 more mins.
11. Enjoy.

Spicy
Lamb Curry

🍲 Prep Time: 15 mins
🕐 Total Time: 1 h 5 mins

Servings per Recipe: 6	
Calories	453 kcal
Fat	30.4 g
Carbohydrates	20.5g
Protein	25.6 g
Cholesterol	90 mg
Sodium	90 mg

Ingredients

1/4 C. cooking oil
3 pods green cardamom
1 pod black cardamom
2 bay leaves
1 cinnamon stick
6 large onions, sliced thin
6 cloves garlic
1 (1/2 inch) piece fresh ginger root, peeled and julienned

2 tsps Kashmiri red chili powder
1 tsp ground cumin
1/2 tsp ground turmeric
salt, to taste
2 tomatoes, pureed
2 lbs lamb chops, rinsed and patted dry
2 tbsps water
3 green chili peppers, halved lengthwise
1/4 C. cilantro leaves, for garnish

Directions

1. Stir fry the following in hot oil until fragrant: cinnamon stick, green and black cardamom, and bay leaves.
2. Now add in the ginger, garlic, and onions.
3. Set the heat to low and continue frying the contents until the onions are brown.
4. Now add your salt, chili powder, cumin, and turmeric.
5. Stir the mix then add in the tomatoes and continue cooking everything for 7 more mins.
6. Add the lamb into the pot and turn up the heat to a medium level. Stir fry everything for about 22 mins then add the some water over everything (only a small amount).
7. Place a lid on the pot and cook the mix for 17 more mins. Take off the cover and add the cilantro and chili peppers.
8. Turn up the heat to a high level and fry the contents for 4 more mins.
9. Enjoy.

ARABIAN
Okra Stew

Prep Time: 20 mins

Total Time: 2 hr 20 mins

Servings per Recipe: 8	
Calories	262 kcal
Fat	8.3 g
Carbohydrates	22.6 g
Protein	21.6 g
Cholesterol	53 mg
Sodium	827 mg

Ingredients

2 tbsps vegetable oil
2 large onions, diced
salt and ground black pepper to taste
2 lbs cubed lamb stew meat
3 tbsps ground cinnamon
1 1/2 tsps ground cumin
1 1/2 tsps ground coriander

1 1/2 tbsps garlic paste
5 (14.5 oz.) cans canned diced tomatoes, drained
1 1/2 tbsps tomato paste
2 beef bouillon cubes
4 C. boiling water
2 lbs frozen sliced okra

Directions

1. Stir fry your onions in veggie oil for a few mins then add in some pepper and salt.
2. Continue frying the onions for 8 more mins until they are browned.
3. Now combine in: the garlic paste, lamb, coriander, cumin, and cinnamon.
4. Let this mix fry for about 12 mins until the lamb is browned.
5. Now add in the tomato paste, and diced tomatoes and fry everything for 7 more mins.
6. At the same time get a bowl and combine your 4 C. of boiling water with your bouillon cubes.
7. Make sure the cubes and water are smoothly combined then add the broth to the lamb with the okra as well.
8. Make sure the okra is submerged in water if not add some more then place a lid on the pot and gently boil everything for 35 mins.
9. Stir the mix at least 3 mins.
10. Now take off the cover and let the mix cook for 50 more mins.
11. Enjoy.

Serbian
Lamb

Prep Time: 10 mins
Total Time: 40 mins

Servings per Recipe: 4
Calories   690 kcal
Fat   46.1 g
Carbohydrates   2.1g
Protein   < 62.8 g
Cholesterol   1223 mg
Sodium   1097 mg

Ingredients

1 1/2 lbs ground turkey
1 lb lean ground beef
1/2 lb ground lamb
1 egg white
4 cloves garlic, minced
1 tsp salt
1 tsp baking soda

2 tsps ground black pepper
1 tsp cayenne pepper
1/2 tsp paprika

Directions

1. Get your grill hot and coat the grate with oil.
2. Get a bowl, combine: egg whites, turkey, ground lamb, and beef.
3. Work the mix with a large wooden spoon then add in: paprika, garlic, cayenne, salt, black pepper, and baking soda.
4. Work the mix again this time with your hands then shape the meat into sausages.
5. Cook the sausages on the grill for 35 mins and turn them frequently.
6. Enjoy.

COUNTRYSIDE
Lamb

🥣 Prep Time: 15 mins
🕐 Total Time: 1 hr 15 mins

Servings per Recipe: 6
Calories   273 kcal
Fat   16.8 g
Carbohydrates   19.3g
Protein   12.4 g
Cholesterol   50 mg
Sodium   912 mg

Ingredients

1 tbsp olive oil
1 medium onion, diced
1 clove garlic, minced
6 medium green bell peppers
2 tbsps diced fresh dill
3/4 tsp salt
1/2 tsp ground allspice
1/2 tsp ground black pepper

1 C. cooked rice
8 oz. ground lamb
1 C. crumbled feta cheese
1 C. tomato sauce
1 C. cold water
1 tbsp fresh lemon juice
1 tsp white sugar

Directions

1. Set your oven to 375 degrees before doing anything else.
2. Stir fry your onions for 7 mins in hot oil then add in the garlic and fry them for 2 more mins.
3. Remove the tops of your peppers and discard the seeds.
4. Place the peppers in a casserole dish with the tops facing upwards.
5. Now get a bowl, combine: pepper, onion mix, allspice, dill, and salt. Stir the mix then add in: feta, lamb, and rice.
6. Stir the mix again to evenly distribute the ingredients and fill your peppers.
7. Get a 2nd bowl, combine: sugar, water, and lemon juice.
8. Cover the tops of your peppers with this mix then pour some into the casserole dish as well.
9. Place a covering of foil on the dish and cook everything in the oven for 50 mins.
10. Remove the foil then continue cooking everything for 20 more mins.
11. Try to baste the peppers and their stuffing with the drippings at least twice.
12. Enjoy.

Lamb
Burgers II

Prep Time: 10 mins
Total Time: 25 mins

Servings per Recipe: 4
Calories	237 kcal
Fat	15.8 g
Carbohydrates	3.1g
Protein	< 20.1 g
Cholesterol	76 mg
Sodium	140 mg

Ingredients

1 lb ground lamb
3 green onions, minced
4 cloves garlic, minced
1 tbsp curry powder
1 tsp ground cumin
1/4 tsp dried red pepper flakes
salt and pepper to taste

Directions

1. Get your grill hot then coat the grate with oil.
2. Get a bowl, combine: pepper, lamb, salt, green onions, red pepper, garlic, cumin, and curry powder.
3. Shape the mix into 4 burgers then cook the burgers on the grill for 6 mins per side.
4. Enjoy.

IRISH
Lamb II

Prep Time: 45 mins
Total Time: 1 hr 10 mins

Servings per Recipe: 4
Calories   476 kcal
Fat   18.1 g
Carbohydrates   51.4g
Protein   27.5 g
Cholesterol   84 mg
Sodium   1529 mg

Ingredients

1 stalk celery, diced
3 carrots, peeled and diced
1 parsnip, peeled and diced
1 small rutabaga, diced
1/4 C. frozen green peas
1 lb ground lamb
1 onion, diced
1 clove garlic, diced

1 (8 oz.) can tomato sauce
1 tsp salt
1/2 tsp ground black pepper
1/4 tsp dried thyme
1/4 tsp dried sage
1/2 C. milk, or as needed
3 C. prepared mashed potatoes
2 tbsps grated Parmesan cheese

Directions

1. Set your oven to 350 degrees before doing anything else.
2. Get a large pot and add the following to it: peas, celery, rutabaga, carrots, and parsnips.
3. Submerge the veggies in about 1 inch of water and get everything boiling.
4. Place a lid on the pot and let the contents gently cook for 17 mins.
5. At the same time being to stir fry your lamb for a few mins then add in the garlic and onions.
6. Continue stir frying everything until the meat is fully done.
7. Now remove any excess oils then add the tomato sauce and cooked veggies. Stir the mix then add: sage, salt, thyme, and pepper.
8. Stir the mix again then place everything into a casserole dish.
9. Combine your potatoes with milk to soften them then layer the potatoes over veggie mix.
10. Top everything with some parmesan.
11. Put everything in the oven for 30 mins.
12. Enjoy.

Lamb Meatloaf

🥣 Prep Time: 15 mins
🕐 Total Time: 1 hr 15 mins

Servings per Recipe: 6
Calories   490 kcal
Fat   27 g
Carbohydrates   37.4g
Protein   23.6 g
Cholesterol   107 mg
Sodium   693 mg

Ingredients

1 1/2 lbs ground lamb
1 egg, beaten
1 small onion, diced
1 C. tomato sauce, divided
1 C. cracker crumbs
salt and pepper to taste
2 tbsps vinegar

2 tbsps prepared mustard
1/2 C. brown sugar
1 C. warm water

Directions

1. Set your oven to 375 degrees before doing anything else.
2. Get a bowl, combine: cracker crumbs, meat, pepper, salt, 1/2 C. tomato sauce, eggs, and onions.
3. Enter the mix into a bread pan.
4. Get a 2nd bowl, combine: water, 1/2 C. tomato sauce, brown sugar, vinegar, and mustard.
5. Combine the mix until the sugar is completely incorporated then coat your lamb with this mix.
6. Cook everything for 65 mins in the oven.
7. Enjoy.

ZUCCHINI
and Lamb

Prep Time: 20 mins
Total Time: 1 hr 10 mins

Servings per Recipe: 4
Calories   649 kcal
Fat   38.7 g
Carbohydrates   38.8g
Protein   40.6 g
Cholesterol   115 mg
Sodium   1523 mg

Ingredients

1 extra large zucchini, halved lengthwise
1 tbsp olive oil
1 sweet onion, diced
1 tbsp diced garlic
1 lb ground lamb
coarse salt to taste
ground black pepper to taste
1 (16 oz.) can tomato sauce

2 tomatoes, diced
3/4 C. crumbled feta cheese
1/2 C. pine nuts
1/4 C. mint leaves
1/4 C. water
1/4 C. mint leaves
3/4 C. seasoned bread crumbs
3/4 C. shredded mozzarella cheese

Directions

1. Set your oven to 450 degrees before doing anything else.
2. Take out the seeds from your zucchini then remove the flesh as well.
3. Throw away the seeds, but keep about an inch of shell from the halves and dice the flesh.
4. Now begin to stir fry your garlic and onions in olive oil for 7 mins then add the lamb and stir fry everything for 9 more mins.
5. Add in the zucchini and stir the mix.
6. Set the heat to low and let everything gently boil for 4 mins.
7. Now remove any excess oils and add in some pepper and salt.
8. Shut the heat and add in: 1/4 C. mint, tomato sauce, pine nuts, feta, and tomatoes.
9. Add this mix into the shells of your zucchini.
10. Place everything in a casserole dish and pour some water into the dish as well.
11. Cook everything in the oven for 35 mins then combine your mozzarella and bread crumbs in a bowl.
12. Top the zucchini with 1/4 C. of mint and then the mozzarella mix.
13. Cook the shells for 12 more mins.
14. Enjoy.

Honey
Chili Lamb

Prep Time: 45 mins
Total Time: 2 hr 45 mins

Servings per Recipe: 4

Calories	616 kcal
Fat	18.4 g
Carbohydrates	82.9g
Protein	39.1 g
Cholesterol	86 mg
Sodium	1135 mg

Ingredients

2 tbsps olive oil
4 lamb shanks
1 onion, diced
2 cloves garlic, minced
2 dried ancho chilis - diced, stemmed and seeded
2 C. chicken broth
4 C. tomato puree
1 tsp ground cumin
1 bay leaf

salt and pepper to taste
6 dried ancho chilis, stemmed and seeded
4 C. boiling water
1/2 C. honey
1 tsp grated orange zest
1 C. plain yogurt
2 tbsps diced fresh cilantro
salt to taste

Directions

1. Set your oven to 350 degrees before doing anything else.
2. Brown all sides of your lamb in a Dutch oven with hot oil then place the meat to the side.
3. Now begin to stir fry your garlic and onions for 4 mins in the same pot then combine in: chicken stock, pepper, cumin, salt, tomatoes, bay leaf, and 2 ancho chilies.
4. Get the mix boiling for 2 mins then add the lamb back in.
5. Place everything in the oven for 2 hrs.
6. Submerge 6 ancho's with boiling water in a bowl. Leave the chilies to sit for 15 mins.
7. Now puree the following: orange zest, chilies, honey, and 2 C. of water.
8. Get a bowl, combine: salt, cilantro, and yogurt.
9. Place a covering of plastic on the bowl and put everything in the fridge.
10. Take your lamb after is it done and put the meat in a roasting pan that has been coated with oil.
11. Place the pan in the oven and turn up the heat to 400 degrees.
12. Top the lamb with the puree and toast everything for 7 mins in the oven.
13. Place the lamb on a serving dish, add some of the tomato mix, and garnish the meat with the yogurt mix.
14. Enjoy.

ARABIAN
Lamb

🥣 Prep Time: 20 mins

🕐 Total Time: 2 hr 20 mins

Servings per Recipe: 5

Calories	586 kcal
Fat	31.5 g
Carbohydrates	33.8g
Protein	42.7 g
Cholesterol	122 mg
Sodium	292 mg

Ingredients

2 tbsps olive oil, divided
2 lbs lamb shanks
1 large onion, quartered
4 cloves garlic, diced
6 C. roma (plum) tomatoes, diced
1 (15 oz.) can chickpeas (garbanzo beans), drained
1 C. cooked lentils

1 tbsp ground cumin
1 tsp ground cinnamon
1/4 tsp ground nutmeg
1/8 tsp crushed red pepper flakes
1 tsp finely diced green chili peppers
1 dash hot pepper sauce

Directions

1. Brown your lamb in 1 tbsp of hot oil then place the meat in a baking dish.
2. Begin to stir fry your garlic and onions until they are soft in the same pan then add in the lentils, chickpeas, and tomatoes.
3. Stir the mix then add: the hot sauce, cumin, chili pepper, cinnamon, pepper flakes, and nutmeg.
4. Stir the mix again and let it cook for 4 mins.
5. Now set your oven to 375 degrees before doing anything else.
6. Take the lamb out of the dish and add the veggie mix to the dish.
7. Layer the lamb over the veggies and place a covering of foil over everything.
8. Cook the mix in the oven for 2 hrs.
9. Enjoy.

Holiday
Lamb

Prep Time: 30 mins
Total Time: 9 hr

Servings per Recipe: 4
Calories   1246 kcal
Fat   79.4 g
Carbohydrates   168.4g
Protein   45.3 g
Cholesterol   192 mg
Sodium   422 mg

Ingredients

2 tbsps olive oil
2 (7 bone) racks of lamb, trimmed, fat reserved
salt and pepper to taste
4 cloves garlic, minced
1 large onion, diced
4 carrots, diced
1 C. celery tops
1 C. fish stock
1 C. beef broth
1 (14.5 oz.) can low-sodium chicken broth

5 sprigs fresh spearmint
3 sprigs fresh rosemary
1 C. mint apple jelly
2 tbsps olive oil
salt and pepper to taste
1 tbsp garlic, minced
1/4 C. panko bread crumbs
2 tbsps olive oil
4 sprigs fresh mint

Directions

1. Get a frying pan and begin to heat the lamb trimmings in 2 tbsps of olive oil.
2. Once the mix is hot add in some pepper and salt.
3. Once the lamb fat is brown, set the heat to low and combine in: the broth, 4 cloves of minced garlic, fish stock, onion, broth, carrots, and celery leaves.
4. Get everything hot then put it all into the crock pot of a slow cooker. Let the mix cook for 8 hrs with low heat.
5. Now run the mix through a strainer into a large pot with a medium level of heat.
6. Add in: mint jelly, rosemary, and spearmint.
7. Add some more broth as well if you feel it is necessary.
8. Simmer the mix until it is syrup like.

9. Place a frying pan in the oven and set it to 450 degrees before doing anything else.
10. Coat your lamb with: garlic, 2 tbsp olive oil, pepper, and salt.
11. Make sure the spices are evenly covering the lamb then coat the meat with your bread crumbs.
12. Take out the hot pan from the oven and add 2 tbsp of olive oil to it.
13. Brown the outsides of the lamb in the hot oil on all sides then place everything back in the oven. Let the lamb cook for 12 mins.
14. Add some of the syrup to a plate for decoration then place some lamb on top.
15. Pour some more syrup on top of the lamb as a garnish with some mint as well.
16. Enjoy.

Lemon Dijon
Lamb Legs

🥣 Prep Time: 15 mins

🕐 Total Time: 1 d 1 hr 35 mins

Servings per Recipe: 6

Calories	922 kcal
Fat	64.6 g
Carbohydrates	13.6g
Protein	67.9 g
Cholesterol	1261 mg
Sodium	631 mg

Ingredients

1/4 C. honey
2 tbsps prepared Dijon-style mustard
2 tbsps diced fresh rosemary
1 tsp freshly ground black pepper
1 tsp lemon zest
3 cloves garlic, minced
5 lbs whole leg of lamb

1 tsp coarse sea salt

Directions

1. Get a bowl, combine: garlic, honey, lemon zest, mustard, black pepper, and rosemary.
2. Stir the mix then add in the lamb and coat it with the mix.
3. Place a covering on the bowl and put everything in the fridge for 8 hrs.
4. Now set your oven to 450 degrees before doing anything else.
5. Top your lamp with salt and lay it on a rack inside a pan for roasting.
6. Cook the lamb in the oven for 25 mins then set the oven to 400 degrees and cook everything for 50 more mins.
7. Enjoy.

GREEK
Souvlaki

Prep Time: 30 mins
Total Time: 1 d 50 mins

Servings per Recipe: 8
Calories   814 kcal
Fat   53.2 g
Carbohydrates   46.5g
Protein   31.1 g
Cholesterol   91 mg
Sodium   766 mg

Ingredients

2 lbs lamb, cut into 1 inch square cubes
1/2 C. olive oil
1 C. broth
1 tsp salt
freshly ground black pepper to taste
1 tsp dried oregano
1 tbsp dried mint, crushed
1 clove garlic, diced
4 C. plain yogurt

1 cucumber, shredded
4 cloves garlic, minced
2 tbsps olive oil
1/2 tsp dried dill weed
salt and pepper to taste
8 pita bread rounds
2 tbsps olive oil
1 red onion, thinly sliced
1 tomato, thinly sliced

Directions

1. Get a bowl, combine: garlic, lamb, mint, half C. olive oil, oregano, pepper, 1 tsp salt, and broth.
2. Stir the mix so the lamb is coated evenly then place a covering of plastic on the bowl and put everything in the fridge for 4 hrs.
3. Now get your grill hot and coat the grate with oil.
4. Get a 2nd bowl, combine: 1 tbsps olive oil, dill, yogurt, pepper, minced garlic, salt, and cucumbers.
5. Stake your lamb onto the skewers then grill the meat for 5 mins.
6. Turn the kebabs and continue grilling them for 5 more mins.
7. Now coat your pieces of pita with olive oil and toast both sides on the grill for 40 secs.
8. Add some tomato and onion inside the pita and serve the stuffed pita with the lamb and dill sauce.
9. Enjoy.

Armenian
Lamb

🥣 Prep Time: 50 mins

🕐 Total Time: 8 h 40 mins

Servings per Recipe: 4

Calories	476 kcal
Fat	16.5 g
Carbohydrates	52.4g
Protein	28.7 g
Cholesterol	76 mg
Sodium	888 mg

Ingredients

1 lb lean ground lamb
1 1/2 C. finely diced onion
1/2 C. diced green bell pepper
1 tsp minced garlic
1 (14.5 oz.) can peeled and diced tomatoes
1 (6 oz.) can tomato paste
1/2 C. diced fresh Italian parsley

1 tsp diced fresh basil
1 tbsp diced fresh mint leaves
1/2 tsp ground cumin
1 pinch cayenne pepper (optional)
4 pita breads, or fluffy tortillas

Directions

1. Stir fry your lamb until almost fully brown, remove an excess oils then add in: garlic, green pepper, and onions.
2. Let the onions fry until they are see-through then add in: cayenne, tomatoes, cumin, tomato paste, mint, parsley, and basil.
3. Let the mix cook for 7 mins then shut the heat and place a lid on the pot.
4. Put everything in the fridge for 8 hrs.
5. Now set your oven to 450 degrees before doing anything else.
6. Equally divide the lamb mix between your tortillas then slice off the edges.
7. Layer everything on a cookie sheet and cook the contents in the oven for 25 mins.
8. Form sandwiches between the pieces of tortillas.
9. Slice the sandwiches into triangles.
10. Enjoy.

LAMB IN
Pakistan

🥘 Prep Time: 35 mins

🕐 Total Time: 2 h 5 mins

Servings per Recipe: 6	
Calories	489 kcal
Fat	35.4 g
Carbohydrates	16.1g
Protein	28.1 g
Cholesterol	88 mg
Sodium	132 mg

Ingredients

4 dried red chili peppers (such as cayenne)
3 long, green fresh chili peppers (such as Indian Jwala)
1 tsp cumin seeds
1 tsp Kashmiri garam masala
1 (1 inch) piece fresh ginger root, peeled and grated
5 cloves garlic, crushed
1/4 C. dried unsweetened coconut
3 tomatoes, diced

6 tbsps vegetable oil
2 large onions, thinly sliced
2 lbs lamb meat, cut into 1 1/2-inch cubes
salt to taste
1/2 tsp ground turmeric
1 C. plain yogurt
1/2 tsp saffron threads
20 whole blanched almonds
1/4 C. diced fresh cilantro

Directions

1. Puree the following: tomatoes, red chilies, grated coconut, green chilies, garlic, cumin, ginger, and masala.
2. Now begin to stir fry your onions, in veggie oil, in a large pot, for 7 mins.
3. Set the heat to low and continue stir frying everything for 12 more mins.
4. Add the chili puree and cook the mix for 4 mins. Then add in the salt and lamb.
5. Stir everything then cook the meat for 10 mins.
6. Now add: almonds, saffron and yogurt.
7. Stir the contents then set the heat to low and let the mix cook for 60 mins.
8. After 60 mins of simmering combine in the cilantro and curry.
9. Enjoy.

Classical
Moroccan Tagine

🥣 Prep Time: 15 mins
🕐 Total Time: 2 h 15 mins

Servings per Recipe: 5

Calories	394 kcal
Fat	14.5 g
Carbohydrates	42.7g
Protein	26.4 g
Cholesterol	71 mg
Sodium	68 mg

Ingredients

1 tbsp olive oil
2 large onions, peeled and sliced into rings
2 lbs lamb meat, cut into 1 1/2 inch cubes
1 tsp ground cumin
1 tsp ground coriander seed
1 tsp ground ginger
1 tsp ground cinnamon

salt to taste
1 tsp ground black pepper
4 pears - peeled, cored and cut into 1 1/2 inch chunks
1/2 C. golden raisins
1/2 C. blanched slivered almonds

Directions

1. Begin to stir fry your onions in oil until tender, in a large pot, then combine in the lamb and brown it.
2. Once the meat is brown add: pepper, cumin, salt, coriander, cinnamon, and ginger.
3. Add in some water to submerge the meat, place a lid on the pot, and let the mix gently boil for 90 mins.
4. After 60 mins of simmering check the mix.
5. If there is too much liquid continue simmering everything without the lid otherwise leave the lid on and keep cooking.
6. Now add in the almonds, raisins, and pears.
7. Let the mix cook for 7 more mins until the fruits are tender.
8. Serve the dish with cooked basmati rice.
9. Enjoy.

ORIENTAL
Lamb

Prep Time: 15 mins
Total Time: 9 h

Servings per Recipe: 10

Calories	325 kcal
Fat	17.7 g
Carbohydrates	13.3g
Protein	27 g
Cholesterol	93 mg
Sodium	688 mg

Ingredients

2/3 C. hoisin sauce
6 tbsps rice vinegar
1/2 C. minced green onions
1/4 C. mushroom soy sauce
4 tbsps minced garlic
2 tbsps honey
1/2 tsp sesame oil
1 tbsp toasted sesame seeds
1/2 tsp ground white pepper

1/2 tsp freshly ground black pepper
1 (5 lb) boneless butterflied leg of lamb

Directions

1. Get a bowl, combine: black pepper, hoisin, white pepper, rice vinegar, sesame seeds, green onions, honey, garlic, and mushroom soy sauce.
2. Stir the mix then add in the lamb and stir everything again. Place a covering of plastic on the bowl and put everything in the fridge for 8 hrs.
3. Now get your grill hot and oil the grate.
4. Grill the lamb for 16 mins per side.
5. Enjoy.

Yogurt-Mint
Lamb Tenderloin

Prep Time: 25 mins
Total Time: 1 h 13 mins

Servings per Recipe: 4
Calories	688 kcal
Fat	57.6 g
Carbohydrates	4g
Protein	36.1 g
Cholesterol	115 mg
Sodium	908 mg

Ingredients

8 6-inch rosemary sprigs
1 tbsp minced garlic
1 tbsp diced fresh thyme
1/3 C. extra virgin olive oil
1/4 C. sherry vinegar
1 tsp sea salt
1 tsp ground white pepper
1 1/2 lbs lamb tenderloin, cut into 2-inch pieces
Salsa Verde:
1/4 C. fresh lemon juice

1/2 C. extra virgin olive oil
1/3 C. Greek yogurt
1 crushed garlic clove
1/4 tsp sea salt
2 tsps diced fresh mint
1 tsp diced fresh oregano
1 tsp diced fresh parsley
1 tsp small capers
1 anchovy filet

Directions

1. Let your rosemary sprigs sit in water for 40 mins.
2. At the same time get a bowl, combine: pepper, garlic, salt, thyme, vinegar, and olive oil.
3. Stir the mix then add in the lamb stir everything again.
4. Place a covering of plastic on the bowl, and put everything in the fridge for 40 mins.
5. Now puree the following: anchovy filet, lemon juice, capers, yogurt, parsley, olive oil, garlic, oregano, salt, and mint.
6. Place this mix to the side.
7. Take your rosemary sprigs and stake the lamb onto them.
8. Grill your lamb skewers on a hot grill coated with oil for 8 mins.
9. When serving the lamb place some of anchovy puree on the side.
10. Enjoy.

ENJOY THE RECIPES?

KEEP ON COOKING
WITH 6 MORE FREE COOKBOOKS!

Click the link below and simply enter your email address to join the club and receive your 6 cookbooks.

http://booksumo.com/magnet

https://www.instagram.com/booksumopress/

https://www.facebook.com/booksumo/

Printed in Great Britain
by Amazon